THREE LITTLE KITTENS.

BY COMUS,

Author of "Mister Fox," &c.

A tale of a cat will here be found,
With three little charming kittens,
And all that they said, and thought, and did,
When they lost—and found—their mittens.

PUBLISHED BY THOMAS NELSON AND SONS,
LONDON, EDINBURGH, AND NEW YORK.

MDCCCLIX.
1859

In the interest of creating a more extensive selection of rare historical book reprints, we have chosen to reproduce this title even though it may possibly have occasional imperfections such as missing and blurred pages, missing text, poor pictures, markings, dark backgrounds and other reproduction issues beyond our control. Because this work is culturally important, we have made it available as a part of our commitment to protecting, preserving and promoting the world's literature. Thank you for your understanding.

THE KITTENS TELLING OF THE LOSS OF THEIR MITTENS.

"THREE LITTLE KITTENS."

"Three Little Kittens."

THREE little kittens they lost their mittens,
 And they began to cry,
   "Oh! mammy dear,
    We sadly fear,
   Our mittens we have lost!"
"What! lost your mittens
You naughty kittens,
   Then you shall have no pie."
    Miew, miew, miew, miew,
    Miew, miew, miew, miew.

The three little kittens they found their mittens,
And they began to cry,
   "Oh! mammy dear,
    See here, see here,
   Our mittens we have found."
"What! found your mittens,
You little kittens,
   Then you shall have some pie."
    Purr, purr, purr, purr,
    Purr, purr, purr, purr.

The three little kittens put on their mittens,
And soon ate up the pie;
   "Oh! mammy dear,
    We greatly fear,
   Our mittens we have soil'd."
"What! soil'd your mittens
You naughty kittens!"
   Then they began to sigh,
    Miew, miew, miew, miew,
    Miew, miew, miew, miew.

The three little kittens they washed their mittens,
And hung them up to dry;
   "Oh! mammy dear,
    Look here, look here,
   Our mittens we have wash'd."
"What! wash'd your mittens,
You darling kittens!
   But I smell a rat close by!
    Hush! hush!" Miew, miew,
    Miew, miew, miew, miew.

THREE LITTLE KITTENS.

> Three little kittens lost their mittens,
> And they began to cry,
> "Oh! mother dear
> We very much fear
> That we have lost our mittens."

So the three little kittens ran to their mother and held up their paws to show that the mittens were really lost. Now, the kittens' mother was a large gray cat. She wore a cap on her head, and a pair of red mittens on her arms. And when she saw the three little kittens sitting before her, with their paws up, and looking half-frightened, half-astonished, she became angry and said "Mee-aow!" Then she sat down before them, looking very fierce, and said, "Mee-aow!" again. At this the three little kittens began to cry, and said they were very sorry indeed for losing them; but they could not tell how it happened, for they were quite sure they had them on when they were eating their breakfast of bread and milk, and that they did not take them off when they went to play.

"But when did you miss them?" asked the cat.

"We don't remember," answered the two eldest kittens.

"Oh! I missed mine just after I went to sleep on the rug," replied the youngest.

At this the other two kittens went into fits of laughter; but their mother gave them each such a slap on the head, and a scratch on the nose that they sat down again trembling before her.

"Come, come; naughty things," she said, "you must not laugh when I am scolding you. It is an easy thing to lose mittens, but not at all easy to find them again. As a punishment I will not speak to you until you have found them. Ah! Miss Spotty, it is all very well to cry, but it would be much better if you never did anything to make you cry, or to oblige me to scold you. Fuff! mee-aow! fuff! I'm very angry."

The cat was silent for a short time, then she said,

"Now, sit still, kittens, do you hear, and wipe your eyes and noses, and listen to me. You are very bad for having lost your mittens. It cost me much money to buy worsted for them, and much time to make them, so, since you have so carelessly,

THE KITTENS ARE SCOLDED.—Page 10

> "Lost your mittens,
> You naughty kittens,
> Then you shall have no pie.
> Mee-aow, mee-aow, mee-aow,
> Go; you shall have no pie.
> Mee-aow, mee-aow, mee-aow."

Their mother said this last "Mee-aow" so fiercely, and followed it up with such an awful "Fuff," that the poor kittens turned round and scampered away as if they were mad, with their hair all standing on end.

Now, the eldest kitten was black; the second was white; and the youngest spotted, so they called each other Blackey and Whitey and Spotty.

"What shall we do?" said Blackey to his sisters when they had fled under a sofa.

"I don't know," said Whitey, and "I don't know," said Spotty.

Blackey shook his head and twirled his tail slowly, and said, "Dear mother is very angry with us. And no wonder, for we had no business to lose our mittens. I'm very, very sorry about it."

"And I'm very sorry too, but I cannot think where we have put them," said Whitey, sadly.

Oh dear me!" sighed Whitey, "I do wish that dear mamma had never made them for us. Of course it was very, very kind of her to do so, but they have given us so much trouble—I really think we should have been much happier without them."

"Hush, hush! my dear sister," said Blackey, "you must not speak that way. You might just as well say you wished we had been made without tails because they give us so much trouble, and are so often caught in the doors and trod on by careless people."

Spotty could hardly speak as she looked up with tears in her eyes and said, "Oh dear! I'm so grieved about the pie!" and she rubbed her stomach gently with her paw.

"What think you," cried Blackey, starting up, "shall we look for them?" So they cried, "Yes, yes," and scampered off to search.

"I'll find them if I should search for a week," said Spotty with a very determined "Mee-aow." And they did search, and found them too. Then they ran joyfully to their mother, waving their mittens in the air, and uttering shouts of a very peculiar kind, which were no doubt intended for hurrahs! although they did not sound very like it.

"Aren't you glad we have found them?" said Blackey.

"Of course I am," replied Spotty, whisking her tail. So,

THE ESCAPE OF THE MOUSE.—Page 14.

THE THREE LITTLE KITTENS GOING TO EAT THE PIE.—Page 16.

> The three little kittens found their mittens,
> And they began to cry
> "Oh! mother dear,
> See here, see here,
> See, we have found our mittens."

The cat received them with a sweet smile and a long, loud "Purr-r-r-r."

"Well, my dear children," she said, "I am glad you have found your mittens, and I hope you will take care not to lose them again."

"Oh yes! dear mother," cried the three kittens "we will take great care of them in future."

The cat smiled and screwed up her whiskers with joy to find that her little ones were so anxious to please her; and then she said,

"Don't you find them nice, useful things, my dears?"

Blackey looked at Whitey and said nothing—but Spotty gave a little jump and said,

"Well, we did'nt think so at first, but I believe they are very nice and useful after all, now I think of it, for they are constantly being lost and keep us employed looking for them, and then they are for ever catching on corners and nails, and making me tumble, which makes Blackey and Whitey laugh very much, and that's funny, you know, if its nothing else!"

Now, while they were so busy talking, a mouse peeped out of its hole, to see if there were any crumbs lying about, and as it saw that the cat and kittens were not watching, it ventured to run a little along the floor. In a moment Spotty caught sight of it. Up went her tail, which grew nearly as thick as her little body, and away she went in pursuit, with her claws out, and her eyes flashing, and her mouth open. Blackey and Whitey and their mother instantly followed; but the little mouse was so quick that it got back in time, and when Spotty crammed her nose and paws into the hole, there was nothing to be found there. Blackey and Whitey each ran against Spotty in their haste, and the cat fell on the top of them all, amid much noise and mee-aowing, which caused the little mouse to laugh, although it trembled a good deal too, when it thought of the danger it had escaped.

When they had recovered from the flutter into which this had thrown them, the cat praised her children; called them good, active, little dears, and said, " No doubt that naughty mouse is laughing at us just now, but never mind, we shall catch it yet, depend upon it, and have it stewed with green pease for supper, my pets; so now,

> "Put on your mittens,
> You silly kittens,
>   And you may have some pie.
>   Purr-r, purr-r, purr-r,
>   Oh! let us have the pie.
>   Purr-r, purr-r, purr-r."

On hearing this, Spotty gave such a sudden scream of delight that her brother and sister jumped five times their own height into the air with the fright, and when they alighted on the ground again, their backs and tails were up, and their hair standing on end, so that they looked like two round balls of fur! "What do you mean by startling us so?" they asked, with an angry little "Fuff."

"Oh! I beg pardon," replied Spotty, looking very meek and innocent, "I did not wish to startle you, but I'm so glad that we are to have the pie after all!" and Spotty was so overjoyed at the thoughts of it, that she gave another scream, made up of a "Purr" and a "Mee-aow" mixed together, and scampered round the room till she was quite out of breath. Blackey and Whitey ran after her all the time; but, although Spotty was very little, and very fat, just like a dumpling, she ran so fast that they could not catch her for five minutes at least.

Then they all rolled together in a lump, so that you would have thought that they were one cat with three heads, and three tails, and six pairs of legs!

Then they separated with a wild cry, and bounced away from each other with their backs up as usual, and their tails very thick, and walking very much sideways, just like crabs, and staring at each other all the time as if they intended to have a very fierce battle.

As they stood thus, Blackey caught sight of his own tail and immediately began to run round after it. Seeing this, Whitey and Spotty rushed at their brother, clasped him in their arms, and they all rolled along the floor again in a knot of confusion, hugging and worrying each other as if they were really angry.

"Let go my tail, Blackey, you rascal," cried Whitey.

"No I wont!" replied Blackey.

"Keep your claws out of my nose, yee-aw! mee-aw! a-a-ow! mee—! spurt! fuff—!" shrieked Spotty.

In the meantime, their mother took up her knitting and looked on with a smile, purring very loudly all the time. At last she called to them to stop; and, when they were seated in a row before her, she told them to go and eat the pie, and said, "Spotty, you little monkey, don't stuff yourself too much!" So,

SPOTTY FALLS INTO THE WASHING TUB.—Page 21

> The three little kittens put on their mittens,
> And soon ate up the pie.
> "Oh! mother dear,
> We greatly fear
> That we have soil'd our mittens."

The pie was a very fine one. It was made entirely of the tails of mice and rat's noses, and was covered with a rich crust of toasted cheese. Besides this, there were a great many different kinds of spices in it. This may, perhaps, surprise you, for it is well known that cats are not fond of spices; but you must remember that the kittens we are speaking of were different from all other kittens in many things. They were fond of spices, so the cat put into the pie a little pepper, a little cinnamon, a little nutmeg, a little ginger, besides a good many cloves and some mustard and a large quantity of canary's claws, and the whiskers of mice.

The moment Spotty saw it she made a rush forward, and would have jumped right into it; but Blackey saw what she was going to do, so he caught her and said in a reproving voice, "My dear sister, you should not be so impatient. Let us all begin to it together. There is no need of hurry."

Spotty blushed deeply and said,

"Oh! dear brother! I'm very foolish, and very sorry,

but——" Spotty could say no more, for at that moment the smell of the crust passed her nose, and, unable to resist it any longer, she burst away from Blackey, rushed up to the pie, and plunged her fore-paws and her nose into the very middle of it! Seeing this, the other two gave a whisk with their tails and did the same, and, in ten minutes, the whole was finished—not so much as the point of a nose or the end of a tail was left. When they had finished and were trying to lick their lips, paws, and whiskers clean, Spotty gave a terrible " Mee-aow," and cried out, " Oh dear me! my mittens are soiled. What will dear mamma say? alas! alas!" The other two also began to cry, for they too had soiled their mittens, so that they were not fit to be seen. But Blackey soon dried his eyes and said, "Let us go and tell mamma, perhaps she wont be angry. At any rate it is better to tell her at once." So they agreed and went and told her. The cat could only hold up her paws in astonishment, and cry, alas! alas!

"Oh dear! oh dear! mee-oo! oo!" cried Blackey.

"I'm very, very sorry, but it was the pie's fault." sobbed Spotty.

Whitey wept in silence.

The cat shook her head and exclaimed, sadly,

"Soil'd your mittens!
You naughty kittens!
Then they began to sigh,
Mee-aow, mee-aow, mee-aow.
Then they began to sigh,
Mee-aow, mee-aow, mee-aow."

It was a sad sight to see these three little kittens, sitting with their mittens all covered over with grease, and the tears rolling down their cheeks; and it was a sad sight to see their poor mother quite unable to speak for sorrow at their foolishness. For, after all, they were really good kittens, and all the evil they did was owing to thoughtlessness. So the cat sighed and said that it was very sad, and the kittens wept more than ever; but Spotty caught sight of Blackey's tail, which was moving at the point, and she could not help making a sudden dart at it. Then she remembered that it was wrong to play when she was naughty, so she sat down and cried again, wiping her eyes with the end of her tail, and looking very wretched.

"Oh! forgive us, dear mother!" said Blackey, "and we will try to behave better in future."

"Forgive us, dear mother!" said Whitey, "and I will never do anything wicked again."

"Forgive us, dear mother!" cried Spotty, and I'll try

all I can to remember not to be naughty. I'll never dirty your ball of worsted by chasing it, and I'll never upset the tea-kettle, and I'll never scratch Blackey's face even in fun, and I'll never grow wild with delight or annoy you any more, and I'll never—never—Oh dear! boo-hoo! I wish I was only good!" and little Spotty put both her paws up to her eyes, and rubbed her face with the soiled mittens, and cried as if her very heart would break.

"Ah! yes, forgive us! do forgive us this time!" they all cried out together.

"I forgive you, my children; but you have made me very miserable;" and the cat shook her head mournfully and sobbed as she went on with her knitting. Now, while she lifted her paw to wipe away a tear, and put her spectacles right, she let fall the ball of worsted which rolled slowly along the floor. In an instant the three kittens forgot their sorrow, rushed after the ball,—Spotty first as usual—and knocked over a small table where stood a beautiful china bowl, and a glass of flowers, which were smashed to atoms. With a general yell they all fled out of the room in extreme terror.

After this the kittens began to think that they might try to wash their mittens;—so,

THEY EAT THE PIE.—Page 18.

THE KITTENS ARE NAUGHTY.—Page 20.

NEW YORK
PUBLIC LIBRARY

ASTOR, LENOX AND
TILDEN FOUNDATIONS
R   L

> The three little kittens washed their mittens,
> And hung them out to dry;
> "Oh! mother dear,
> Do you not hear,
> That we have washed our mittens."

These kittens were very determined little creatures, and when they had once made up their minds that a thing ought to be done, they always did it in spite of all difficulties; so they resolved to wash the mittens. Whitey laughed at their troubles, and Blackey laughed too, but as the soap-suds made his eyes smart and water very much, it just seemed as if he were crying and laughing at the same time, and this looked so funny that Whitey laughed till she nearly cried, and let her mittens fall into the water two or three times.

They washed them in a small tub; and much difficulty they had in doing it. The sides of the tub were so high that Blackey and Whitey were scarcely able to reach the water, and Spotty was so small that she had to climb up and stand on the edge of it, while she put down her paws to wash. Then Whitey said she couldn't hold the soap, it was so slippery; and some more suds went into Blackey's eyes and made him nearly blind; and the soap was lost in the water two or three times, and they had great difficulty in finding it again. All this time Spotty was sitting on the edge of the tub, washing very busily, when Blackey said, "Take care, Spotty, you will fall in if you don't mind."

"No fear!" cried Spotty; but, just as she said so, down she went, head first and tail last, and when she recovered her feet again and stood up on her hind legs, her eyes staring with fright, and her mouth gasping for breath, she looked so funny, covered all over with soapsuds, that the other kittens laughed very much and then cried, after which they pulled her out of the tub. But this was no easy thing to do—and then when they did get her out, they rubbed her with a towel, and held her up to the fire to dry; but they were so stupid that they singed the point of her tail very badly! However they got her dried at last, and dried their mittens also.

"Now, darling," said Whitey, giving Spotty a kiss, "do you feel better? are you quite dry?"

"Of course she is," said Blackey, pulling her tail slily.

When all was ready they took the mittens in their paws and ran joyfully with them to the cat, who was still at her knitting, looking very sad indeed. When she saw what they had done she exclaimed with pleasure and surprise,

"Washed your mittens!
Oh! you're good kittens;
  But I smell a rat close by,
    Hush! hush! mee-aow, mee-aow,
  We smell a rat close by,
    Mee-aow, mee-aow, mee-aow."

As she spoke, a rat sprang out of its hole, rushed across the room, along the passage, and out into the garden. The cat instantly threw down her knitting, tossed her spectacles into the fire, jumped over the heads of her children, and dashed away in chase of the rat, while the three little kittens dropt their mittens and followed her as fast as their little legs could wag, mee-aowing wildly as they went, and tumbling over the window in their haste; so that Spotty fell flat on her back, and Whitey fell into Spotty's arms, and Blackey fell on the top of them both. But they soon scrambled up again and then they saw the cat standing at the mouth of a hole into which the rat had run.

They all stood watching the hole for a good long time, for they knew that the rat did not live there, and that it was not a comfortable hole at all, being not very deep and rather damp, so that it was likely the rat would catch cold if it remained long there. The cat stood near the hole to be ready to pounce on the rat the moment it should show its nose, and the three kittens stood a little way behind her, looking on very anxiously.

"I wish very much," said Whitey, "that we could catch a rat, I think the three of us might manage to kill it easily."

"Oh!" whispered Spotty as her eyes opened wide with surprise, "just look at mamma's tail! such a size!"

"Just look at your own," said Blackey, "it's not much less!"

Spotty turned her head to look at it, but at that moment the rat rushed out of the hole, and her mother flew off after it. The kittens immediately followed, and away they went over fields, and hedges, and ditches; with their eyes flashing, their tails up, and their hair on end. So the rat, and the cat, and the three little kittens fled out of sight, and never were heard of more!

THE WHOLE FAMILY GIVE CHASE TO A RAT.—Page 24.

✓

Printed by Libri Plureos GmbH in Hamburg, Germany